NAMI

THE CORNISH

Three Hundred Cornish First Names

DYLLANSOW TRURAN

First published by Dyllansow Truran 1984

This edition 1999: Dyllansow Truran,
Croft Prince, Mount Hawke, Truro TR4 8EE

Illustrations & cover Sue Lewington
Main text set in Fenice 10/12pt
Design Ray Lancefield, The Design Field

Printed & bound in Cornwall
R Booth (Bookbinder) Ltd & Troutbeck Press
Antron Hill, Mabe, Penryn TR10 9HH

ISBN 1 85022 122 7

Introduction

••

This book has been prepared to help parents with the practical task of choosing distinctively Cornish first names for their children. It has been in print in various forms since 1970 and its success is demonstrated by the number of children, some now adults, living in Cornwall and beyond who bear names provided by this book.

To compile a list of names of Cornish origin is not an easy matter. The Norman conquest came only a century or so after Cornwall's annexation by England and it seems that after this time many of the old Christian names of Celtic origin were replaced by ones of Norman origin, at least for the official record. It is highly likely however that many of the old names continued in vernacular Cornish.

How then does one compile a list of Cornish first names? One very interesting document is known as the Bodmin Manumissions. This document, formerly the property of Bodmin Priory and now in the British Museum, was written at the beginning of the 10th century and contains a list of names of slaves given their freedom by their masters. This list contains about 150 names of Cornish origin.

Another source are the historical Cornish manuscripts, miracle plays, translations of parts of the Bible, a folk tale, sermons and various other short pieces. In addition there is evidence that Cornish saints' names were used as Christian names up until the 19th century. The early parish registers suggest that although it was perhaps more usual for a child to take the name of the saint of his own parish, this was not an invariable rule. The names of the better-known saints, PETROK and GERENS for example, seem to have a fairly wide distribution in central and western Cornwall. Occasionally the saint's name was given a feminine form, e.g. COLUMBA for COLUM, to make it suitable for bestowal on girls. Many Cornish names can be deduced from place names. The Cornish 'Tre' - homestead is often followed by the personal name of the original owner. It must be remembered however that the first letter of that name has sometimes undergone a change (lenition) following the word 'Tre'.

In addition to the names of Cornish/Celtic origin a few have been added which have been popular in Cornwall over many centuries whereas their use has diminished in other parts of the British Isles.

Spelling

••

The aim has been to keep a middle course. As far as possible, all Celtic names are spelt in accordance with Middle Cornish principles, but this aim has not been followed blindly, especially when it has seemed likely to lessen the attractiveness of a name for modern users. In general, saints' names are given their more Cornish medieval spellings. The Old Cornish -OC in names like Petroc has given way to -OK for three reasons. The first of these is that -OC is used in the anglicised rendering of Welsh names ending in OG; the second is that final -C has been foreign to Cornish spelling since the Old Cornish period; and the third is that final -C has an archaic (or Welsh) appearance. THE SPELLINGS ARE SUGGESTED ONES ONLY, for there are no hard-and-fast conventions governing the spelling of Cornish names. It is better for names like PETROK to be anglicised as PETROCK (the usual spelling adopted by earlier generations of users) than not used at all. If parents dislike the appearance of the Y retained in some Cornish names, they are at liberty to use a more modern I. Some may prefer to use a Z in place of an S in a Cornish name, bearing in mind that, except when an initial, a Cornish S is invariably pronounced Z.

Professional students of the Celtic languages, Cornish historians, hagiologists and other specialists are reminded of the title of this booklet; it sets out to provide NAMES FOR THE CORNISH - nothing more. While every care has been taken in the compilation of the list, inconsistencies and questionable etymologies are bound to have crept in.

A Note on Pronounciation
••

The stress or accent in a Cornish word of two syllables is normally put on that before the last, as in Cornish placenames. The 'imitated pronunciation' used in the list indicates stress by the use of capital letters. For example, the placename TRENOWETH would be rendered 'Tre-NOW-eth'. When a word is not accompanied by its 'imitated pronunciation', it may be assumed that it is pronounced like a similarly spelt English word. EXCEPT WHEN AN INITIAL, and in the combination, SS, S in CORNISH NAMES has the SOUND OF Z.

Symbols & Abbreviations
••

+	indicates that it cannot be regarded as distinguishingly Cornish.
D	indicates that a name is not traditional and that it has been taken from a Cornish dictionary.
PN	the capital letters PN indicate that a respelt Old Cornish name seems to be found as a place name element, but that it does not seem to be attested in other sources.
RS	= respelt and occurs in phrases like 'RS Old Cornish name'. (It was felt that it would be misleading to describe such names as bare 'Old Cornish' names).

Bod. man. = Bodmin Manumissions.

NAMES FOR BOYS

+ALAN

A Celtic name of doubtful etymology. The name of an obscure Breton saint who gave his name to St. Allen, near Truro, ALAN was introduced into England as a whole by Breton followers of William the Conqueror. ALAN has since become so common that its connection with Cornwall is usually overlooked. The spellings ALLAN and ALLEN are not supported by Breton and early Cornish tradition.

ALWAR

(Pron. 'al-WORE') The name of a traditional Cornish king in the play 'Bewnans Meryasek', but apparently not an Old Cornish name at all. It is probably the Old English name AELFWARU which Eilert Ekwall (Oxford Dictionary of English Placenames) sees in the Madron placename ALVERTON (ALWARTON 1229), 'Alwar's homestead'.

ARTHEK

PN - RS Old Cornish name = the Old Welsh name ARTHWG, a derivative of ARTH, 'bear'.

+ARTHUR

The name of the semi-historical British freedom fighter who has a special place in the memory of the Cornish. The etymology of the name has been the subject of much dispute; it may be derived from British ARTOS, 'bear', but is more probably of Latin origin. Like ALAN, ARTHUR is too common to be distinguishingly Cornish.

ARTHYEN

PN - RS Old Cornish name = the Old Welsh name ARTHIEN, from British ARC-TOGENOS, 'bear born'.

AUSTOL

A Breton saint who gave his name to St. Austell.

+BASTIAN

Latin SEBASTIANUS, 'man of Sebastia' (a city). A shortened form of SEBASTIAN not uncommon in 16th century Cornwall. Essentially a French and Spanish name.

+BAWDEN or BOWDEN

Old German BALDAVIN, a compound of BALDA, 'bold', and VINI, 'friend'. BAWDEN, fairly common in Cornwall up to the 17th century, is from BAUDOIN, the Norman-French form of BALDWIN.

BENESEK

(Pron. 'be-NEZZ-ek') RS Old Cornish name from Latin BENEDICTUS, 'blessed', found as a Bod. man. name and as a possible placename element.

BRANEK or BRANOK

PN - RS Old Cornish name found in a number of placenames.

BRANWALATHER
(Pron. 'bran-wol-LATH-er') Some authorities believe that St. Branwalather, about whom nothing is known, is honoured at St. Breward. The name means 'raven leader'.

BRENGY
(Pron. 'BREEN-gee') RS Old Cornish name found in the Bod. man. and as an element in several placenames. The name means 'noble dog'.

BRYOK or BREOK
(Pron. 'bree-OK') A Welsh saint who gave his name to St. Brieuc in Brittany and to St. Breock in Cornwall. The name is from British BRIGACOS.

BUTHEK, BITHEK, or BUDOK
(Pron. The 'th' like the soft 'th' in 'that') A Breton saint who gave his name to the parish of Budock, near Falmouth. BUDOC(K) is the anglicised Old Cornish form of the name, which occurs in its Middle Cornish form BUTHEK in medieval sources and is partly preserved in the surname BIDDICK. BITHEK is a suggested spelling with modern use in mind. BUTHEK which means 'victorious', is the masculine form of the name of the famous Queen Budhycca (Boadicea) who led a revolt against the Romans. The name occurs in the Bod. man.

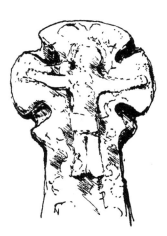

CADAN
PN - RS Old Cornish name = the Old Welsh name CADAN.

CADRETH
PN - RS Old Cornish name = the Old Welsh name CADREITH.

CADOR
A legendary ruler of Cornwall. Old Cornish CADWUR, 'warrior'.

CARANTOK
(Pron. 'car-RANT-OK') A Welsh saint who gave his name to Crantock, near Newquay, and to several other places in Wales and Brittany. The names seems to be a derivative of the root CARANT, 'love'.

CARASEK or CARADOK
(Pron. 'car-RAZZ-ek'/'car-RADD-OK') The name of a legendary Duke of Cornwall and of a famous chieftain, Caractacus, who was taken to Rome as a prisoner in the 1st century AD. The name means 'amiable'. Since CARADWG is a favourite Christian name in Wales, there is everything to he said for preferring CARASEK, the distinctively Cornish medieval placename form of the name.

CASEK or CADOK

(Pron. 'cazz-ek'/'cadd-OK') A common place-name element. St. Cadoc, one of the most famous of Welsh saints, may have visited Cornwall, where the well-known chapel at Harlyn Bay hears his name. Middle Cornish CASEK is more 'Cornish' and is unlikely to be confused with Welsh CADOG.

CASVELYN

(Pron. 'caz-VELL-an') Found as the name of a traditional Cornish petty king in the play 'Bewnans Meryasek'. A native Celtic name, it may derive from British CATU-BELINUS.

CASWAL

(Pron. 'cazz-woll') An RS Old Cornish name meaning 'battle powerful'.

CASWORON

PN (Pron. 'cazz-WORR-an' - rhymes with the place-name 'Gorran') RS old Cornish name meaning 'battle hero'.

CASWYN

PN (Pron. 'cazz-win') RS Old Cornish name from British CATUUINDOS, 'fair battle'.

CATHNO(W)

PN (Pron. 'cath-noo') RS Old Cornish name = the Old Welsh name **CADNOU**, 'battle-known'.

CLEMO(W)

(Pron. 'clemm-O') A Cornish O-suffix pet-form of CLEMENT. The Cornish historian Carew (1555-l62O) gives CLEMMOWE as the Cornish firstname equivalent of standard English CLEMENCE/CLEMENT.

CLESEK

PN (Pron. 'clezz-ek') RS Old Cornish name = the Old Welsh name CLODOC, from British KLUT-, 'famous'.

CLETHER

(Pron. to rhyme with 'leather') Apart from the appearance of his name in the Cornish list of the Children of Brychan, nothing is known about the saint who gave his name to St. Clether in Cornwall and to Cleder in Brittany.

COLAN

(Pron. rhyme with 'pollen') A Celtic saint who gave his name to Colan, near Newquay. He is probably the saint whose name is perpetuated in Llangollen in Wales and in Langolen in Brittany. As a Cornish Christian name, COLAN is found up the end of the 17th century.

COLUM

(Pron. 'cull-um') A Celtic missionary who, despite tradition to the contrary, was probably a man. The name, like Irish COLUM/COLM, is from Latin COLUMBA, 'dove'. Used up to 1610 as a name for boys born in the parish of St. Columb, but also found later elsewhere.

CONAN

(Pron. 'conn-an' and not like the name of the author, Conan Doyle) The name of a semi-historical Cornish king and of an authentic 10th century Bishop of Cornwall. A fairly common placename element and possibly the real name of the patron of Roche, St. Gonand. CONAN = Old Welsh CYNAN, Old Breton CONAN and Irish CONAN.

CORENTYN

(Pron. 'cawr-RENT- in') A Breton saint, honoured as first bishop of Cornouaille and associated with the Cornish parish of Cury.

CORNELLY

(Pron. 'cawr-NELL-ee') The church of this name near Tregony seems to he dedicated to CORNELIUS, Bishop of Rome, who is venerated as a martyr.

COSTENTYN

(Pron. 'coss-STENT-in') The Cornish form of CONSTANTINE (Welsh CYSTENNIN), the name of the first Christian emperor. There was also a Cornish St. Constantine who, according to tradition, abandoned his kingdom to become a monk. His name lives on in Constantine (earlier Langostentyn), near Falmouth, and in Constantine Bay near Padstow. In its anglicized form CONSTANTINE the name was not uncommon in Cornwall up to about the middle of the 18th century.

CUBERT

(Pron. 'kew-bert') Cubert, near Newquay, is believed to take its name from an obscure Celtic saint whose name may account for the Cardiganshire placename GWBERT. There are records of the use of the saint's name as a Cornish Christian name.

CUBY

see KEBY.

DAVETH

The Cornish form of the scriptural name DAVID. Occurs in Cornish literary sources and = the Welsh name DAFYDD.

+DAVY
A pet-form of DAVID not uncommon in pre-18th century Cornwall. The surnames DAVIE and DAV(E)Y are chiefly Cornish and Devonian.

DÉ or DAY
(Pron. 'day') A British saint who gave his name to St Day, near Redruth. Some authorities identify him with the St. Dei venerated in Brittany.

DEGYMAN
(Pron. 'de-GIMM-an') St. Degyman (DECUMAN) was venerated at Watchet in Somerset and in South Wales, where the chapel at LLANDDEGYMAN, Breconshire, bore his name. In Cornwall it seems to occur in the place-name DEGIBNA, Helston, allegedly the site of a medieval chapel dedicated in his honour. The name is ultimately from Latin DECUMANUS, 'a farmer of tithes'.

DENZIL
Popular in Cornwall over a long period.

DEWY
A Cornish form of the scriptural name DAVID found as a Bod. man. name and as a placename element; e.g as the old name for Davidstow, 'Dewstow'.

+DIGORY
Possibly from the French ÉGARÉ, 'strayed', DIGORY seems to go back to the medieval romance of 'Sir Degore'. Although found elsewhere, DIGORY came to be regarded as mainly Cornish. Obsolete or rare since the end of the last century.

DONYERTH or DONYARTH
A Primitive Cornish name reconstructed from the inscription on the well-known cross base with Hiberno-Saxon interlacings at St. Cleer. The inscription reads: DONIERT ROGAUIT PRO ANIMA, 'Doniert ordered this stone for the good of the soul'. This Doniert may have been the same person as the semi-historical DUNGARH, King of Cornwall. Whatever the connection, the approximate pronunciation of the two names would have been 'donn-YERTH' and 'donn-YARTH'. Cf. the Old Welsh name DUNGARH, from British DUBNOGARTOS.

EDERN
PN RS Old Cornish name = the Old Welsh name EDEYRN and the Old Breton name EDERN, from Latin AETURNUS.

ELEDER
PN - RS Old Cornish name = the Old Welsh name ELIDIR.

ELWYN
St. Elwyn is said to have been one of a band of Irish saints who landed in Cornwall in the 5th century. A chapel at Sithney records his name and the modern church at

Hayle is dedicated in his honour. St. Elwyn's written Life existed at Breage in 1538 but has not survived.

ENODER

An obscure Celtic saint who gave his name to St. Enoder, near Newquay. There are several records of the use of ENODER as a Christian name.

ENODOK

(Pron. 'enna-DOK') An obscure Celtic saint who gave his name to St. Enodoc, near Padstow. He was honoured during the Middle Ages at Bodmin Priory as St. WENE-DOC. The name could be restored as GWENEDOK.

ENYON

The name of a legendary ruler of Cornwall = the Old Welsh name EINEON, from late Latin ANNIANUS.

ERBYN

PN - A man named ERBYN was said to have been the father of St. Selevan.

ERVAN

The name-saint of the parish of St. Ervan. Although the present dedication is to St. Hermes, it seems likely that the man behind the name bore a British name like *ERMIN- or *ARMIN-.

EVAL

(Pron. to rhyme with 'revel' and not 'evil') A saint who is no more than a bare name. It is possible that EVAL is from Latin HUMILIS, from which is derived the Cornish word HUVEL, 'humble'.

FEOK

(Pron. 'fee-OK') St. Feok is assumed to have been a man, but in Latin references of the Middle Ages the name has the feminine form FEOCA. Prof. Loth regarded the name as a corruption of MAEOC. In Finistere St. Maeoc is eponym of the parish of Lanveoc, a name practically identical with the LAFEAGE or LA FEOCK near Feock church. The Cornish surname VAGUE/VAGE, which derives from this parish, preserves the older pronunciation of FEOK, 'fay-ok' or 'fay-ek'. Cf. the name MAYEK/MAYOK.

FRYEK or FRYOK

(Pron. 'free-ek' / 'free-OK') An RS Bod. man. name and a placename element = the Old Welsh name FRIOC, perhaps from FRI 'nostril'.

+GAWEN

(Pron. 'gaou-en') One of the most famous of the Arthurian knights, nephew of King Arthur; and probably the original hero of the Grail quest. He appears in the Welsh TRIADS and the MABINOGION as 'Gwalchmei'. It is believed that GAWEN (Gawain,

Gawayne and Gavain are Frenchified spellings) is a genuine Welsh name corresponding to an Old Breton name GAUEN found in UUOI-GAUAN.

GENNYS
A little-known Celtic saint whose name is perpetuated in St. Gennys, near Bude.

GERENS
(Pron. 'gerr-anz') The Cornish form of the well-known Welsh name GERAINT, from British GERONTIUS. According to legend, St. Gerens, who is patron of Gerrans, was a king of Cornwall. It seems likely that legend had confused him with an authentic early Cornish petty king of the same name. There are many records of the use of the name GERENS as a Cornish Christian name.

GERMO(GH)
An obscure, possibly Irish, saint who gave his name to Germoe, near Helston. The name is from Latin GERMOCHUS.

GLEWAS or GLEWYAS
(Pron. to rhyme with the surname 'Lewis') A British saint, probably from Wales, who gave his name to St. Gluvias, near Penryn. The name may be a derivative of GLEW, 'clear', 'bright'. The forms GLEWYAS/GLEWYATH of medieval documents survive in the Cornish surname GLUYAS. Cf. the name BUTHEK.

GORGANS
(Pron. 'gawr-GANZ') An RS Bod. man. name and a placename element = the Old Welsh name GUORCANT, from British VOR-CANTOS, 'very white / splendid'.

GORHEDER
PN(Pron. 'gawr-HEDD-er') A placename and a RS Bod. man. name = the Old Welsh name GUORHITIR, from British VOR-SETROS, 'very bold'.

GORLAS
(Pron. 'gawr-luz') The Gorlois of Arthurian legend and a placename element. GORLAS corresponds to the Old Welsh name GOR-LOES and the Old Breton name UUORLOIES, and may mean 'very pure / holy'.

GORNEVES
PN (Pron. 'gawr-NEVV-uz') RS Old Cornish name the Old Welsh name GURNIVET, from British VOR-NEME-TOS, 'very holy'.

GORON

(Pron. to rhyme with 'foreign') A Celtic saint who gave his name to Gorran, near Mevagissey. There is also a St. Guron's well at Bodmin. The name means 'hero'. Cf. CASWORON.

GORTHELYK

(Pron. 'gawr-THEL-ik' (with the 'th' soft as in 'then') RS Bod. man. name - the Old Welsh name GURDILIC, 'very beloved'.

GOURGY

(Pron. 'goor-gee') RS Bod. man. name and a placename element. The name means 'man dog'.

GRYFFYN

This name is found in the Cornwall Domesday and in a late 14th century Cornish literary source. Regarded by Christian name investigators as a diminutive or alternative form of GRIFFITH, GRIFFIN occurs in the Middle Ages in counties bordering Wales and has since given rise to an uncommon but fairly widely distributed surname.

GRIFYUTH or GRIFFUTH

(Modern pron. as in the surname 'Griffith') RS Bod. man. name = the Old Welsh name GRIPHIUD, now spelt GRUFFUDD, and frequently anglicized as GRIFFITH. The second element is IUTH, 'lord'.

GWALATHER

PN ('gwoll-LATH-ur') Rs Old Cornish name = the Old Breton name UUALATR, 'leader'.

GWENDERN

RS Bod. man. name meaning 'white / splendid lord'. The last element in the name, TEGERNO- 'lord', is also the last element in the Cornish word for 'king', 'myghtern'. Although the church at Wendron is now dedicated to a female WEN-DRONA, it seems likely that the real name-saint of the parish was one GWENDERN, an otherwise unknown Cornish, Breton or Welsh male missionary. From 1500 to about 1800 the placename Wendron is often found as Gwendron, its more Cornish form.

GWITHYEN

(Pron. with the 'th' soft as in 'then') Nothing is known about the saint whose name is perpetuated in Gwithian, near Hayle. A name corresponding to the Old Breton name UUETHIEN seems to occur in at least two Cornish placenames.

GWELESYK

PN (Pron. 'go-LEZZ-ik') RS Old Cornish name = the Old Breton name UUOLETIC, a derivative of GWLAS, 'nation'.

GWORYEN
PN - RS Old Cornish name = the Old Breton name UUORIEN, from British VOR-GENOS.

GWYDEL
PN (Pron. to rhyme with 'fiddle') RS Old Cornish name - the Old Welsh name GUI-TAL, from Latin VITALIS.

GWYNHELEK
PN (Pron. 'gwinn-HEL-lik') RS Old Cornish name = the Old Breton name UUIN-HAELOC, from UUIN, 'white / splendid' and HAELOC, a derivative of HAEL, 'gener-ous'.

GWYNEK or GWYNOK
St. Gwynok, who may have been a Welshman, lived after the 'Age of the Saints'. About the year 700 he helped to found a monastry in Flanders. In Cornwall his name, which means 'little fair one', is associated with the parish of St. Winnow, and is found in several placenames.

GWYNOW
PN (Pron. 'gwinn-O') RS Old Cornish name = the Old Breton name UUINOU, prob-ably a derivative of UUIN, 'fair / splendid'.

GWYNWALLO(W)
(Pron. 'gwinn-WOLL-O') The great British saint who founded the famous monastery of Landevennec in Brittany. Landewednack (earlier Landewenek) is the same name, and nearby Gunwalloe (earlier Gwynwalla) preserves the name of the saint himself. GWYNWALLO(W) = the Old Breton name UUINUUOLO.

GWYNYER
According to a Life of St. Gwynyer written 800 years after his death, he was the leader of a party of Irish migrants murdered by the pagan King Teudar. He may have been a Welsh missionary. His name apparently = Welsh GUINIER and Breton GUIGNER.

GWYTHENEK
(Pron. 'gwa-THEN-ek') The name of a saint honoured in Brittany and Cornwall. There are indications that St. Gwythenek was one of the earlier saints, and that his cult at Padstow and Bodmin diminished following the arrival of St.Petrok. His monastic close, LAN WETHINOC, became the first recorded name for what is now Padstow, and as late as the 16th century the old name survived in the form LODENEK as the true Cornish name for the town. GWYTHENEK is found in at least two placenames.

GWYTHERYN
PN (Pron.'gwith-THERR-in') RS Old Cornish name = the Old Welsh name GWYTHERIN.

+HANNIBAL

Phoenician, the name of the great Carthaginian general. Although essentially an Italian name, Hannibal came into use in 16th century Cornwall. Almost exclusively Cornish in distribution ever since. Rare or obsolete for over a century.

+HARVEY

Is probably from HERVE, the French form of Breton HAERVEU, the name of a favourite Breton saint and poet. The name, a compound of Old Breton AER 'carnage' and -UIU 'worthy', was introduced into England at the time of the Conquest and soon became quite common. It became unfashionable in the 14th century and was in rare use until the 19th century. The name has been included because of its Breton associations.

+HEDLEY

Popular in Cornwall over a long period.

HEDREK or HEDROK

PN (Pron.'hedd-rek'/'hedd-DROK') RS Old Cornish name = the Old Breton name HEDROC, a derivative of HEDR, 'bold'. Possibly the name-saint of Lanhydrock, about whom nothing is known.

HENNA

Apparently a 'Cornish' pet-form of HENRY.

HICCA

A 'Cornish' pet-form of RICHARD; the equivalent of 'Hick' or 'Dick'.

HORNWALLON

(Pron. 'horn-WOLL-un') RS Old Cornish name from the Bodmin Manumissions, from British ISARNOUALLANOS.

+HOWEL

The Breton name HOEL, corresponding to the Welsh name HYWEL, 'eminent', was used from time to time in England during the Middle Ages. Although found as the name of medieval Cornishmen (e.g. Howel de Cruglas, Member of Parliament for Bodmin in 1327), there is no evidence that its use represented the survival of a native Cornish equivalent of HYWEL / HOEL.

+HOCKEN

Hocken, found in early parish registers, is still used as a genuine Christian name by at least one Cornish family. It is presumably the obsolete name HALKIN, the diminutive of HAL, a favourite pet-form of HENRY.

JACCA

A 'Cornish' equivalent of JACK.

JAGO

A British form of JAMES, from Latin JACOBUS, found as a placename element and surviving in the modern surname. It corresponds to Welsh IAGO, and like all other Cornish names ending in O, it has no connection whatever with Spain.

JAMMA

An earlier 'Cornish' pet-form of JAMES. Various 17th century sources indicate that JAMES was pronounced JAMMEZ by contemporary Cornishmen.

JEFFRA

A pre-17th century colloquial form of GEOFFREY. Middle English GEFFREY seems to represent two, if not three, Old German names, the second element in all of which is FRITHU, 'peace'. Cf. Welsh SIEFFRE.

JENKEN

Seventeenth century Christian name connected to the surname Jenkin.

JERMYN or GERMAN

Latin GERMANUS, 'a German'. Although found outside Cornwall, the name's former popularity among Cornishmen may have owed something to the fact that St. Germanus of Auxerre is patron of St. Germans and Rame.

JORY

Is thought to be a pet-form of GEORGE, for which it is used by modern writers in Cornish.

+ JOSE

A common medieval name used for both men and women in the forms JOSSE, GOCE, etc. Along with the O-suffix names it gave further substance to legends about Spanish influence on Cornwall. It has no connection whatever with Spanish JOSE and seems to be the name of a 7th century Breton saint, JODOC, son of JUDI-CAEL, a hermit of Ponthieu. As a man's name JOSE died out in the 14th century; as a woman's name it was virtually obsolete when revived in the 1900s in the form JOYCE.

JOWAN

The Cornish form of JOHN, like Old Welsh JOUAN, Old Breton IOUUAN, from Latin JOHANNES by way of British. The earlier pronunciation rhymed with the surname 'Owen', but by the 17th century the name was pronounced 'JOOAN', the spelling used by the Cornish writer Nicholas Boson.

KÉ, KEA or KAY

(Pron. 'Kay') A British saint who gave his name to Kea, near Truro. According to

Breton legend, St. Ké founded a monastery at Cleder and later returned to Britain to try and make peace between King Arthur and Modred. The name is said to be from Latin CAIUS.

KEBY or CUBY

(Pron. 'kebb-ee'/ 'kew-bee') According to tradition, St. Keby was actually Cornish-born, the son of St. Selevan. He is patron of Duloe and Tregony. Early spellings of his name, allied to evidence from Wales, show that CUBY is corrupt.

KENAL

PN (Pron. to rhyme with 'kennel') RS Old Cornish name = the Old Welsh name CYN-HAEL, from the British CUNOSAGLOS, 'generous chief'. KENNAL is found twice as an early 16th century Christian name, but it seems likely to be for the surname KENALL.

KENAN

PN form of CONAN resulting from vowel reduction. See CONAN.

KENBRES

PN (Pron. 'kenn-brez') RS Old Cornish name = the Old Breton name CONBRIT and the Old Welsh name CYNBRYD.

KENEDER

PN (Pron. 'ke-NEDD-ur') RS Old Cornish name = the Old Welsh name CYNIDR, from British CUNO-SETROS, 'bold chief'.

KENDERN

PN - RS Old Cornish name = the Old Welsh name CYNDEYRN, from British CUNO-TIGERNOS, 'chief lord'.

KENGAR

St. Kengar was venerated in Wales and Brittany and a chapel at Lanivet bore his name. The unreduced form of the name is almost certainly evident in the place-name TREGONGER and = the Old Breton name CONGAR.

KENHEBRES

PN (Pron. 'ken-HEBB-riz') RS Old Cornish name = the Old Welsh name CONHIBRIT.

KENHORN

PN - RS Old Cornish name = the Old Welsh name CYNHAERN, from CUNO-ISARNOS, 'iron chief'. Occurs in the placename Linkinhorne (LAN KENHORN), 'monastic enclosure (of) Kenhorn', and is the last element in the well-known Cornish surname POLKINHORN.

KENOW
PN (Pron. 'kenn-o') RS Old Cornish name = the Old Welsh name CENAU and the Old Breton name CANAO, from British CONOUIOS. Its literal meaning seems to be 'cub'.

KENVER
PN - RS Old Cornish name = the Old Welsh name CYNFOR, probably from British CUN-MORUS, 'great chief'. According to the 19th century Life of St. Paul Aurelian, King Mark of Cornwall was also known by the name of CONOMOR.

KENWAL
PN (Pron. 'Kenn-woll') RS Old Cornish name = the Old Welsh name CYNWAL, from British CUNO-UALLOS, 'powerful chief'. Cognate with the Irish name CONALL.

KENWYN
PN - RS Old Cornish name = the Old Welsh name CENWYN, from CUNO-UINDOS, 'white / splendid chief'. Possibly the name-saint of Kenwyn, Truro, though early spellings of this placename suggest that it may mean 'white ridge'.

KENWYTHEN
PN (Pron. 'kenn-WITH-en') RS Old Cornish name = the Old Welsh name CONGUETHEN and the Old Breton name KENGUETHEN, from CUNO-, 'high / lofty' and a derivative UUETH, 'battle'.

KEVERN
Nothing is known about the saint who gave his name to St. Kevern. His name appears to he a corruption of some name like AKEVRAN. It has been suggested that it is Irish AED COBHRAN. KEVERN has been used as a Christian name.

KITTO(W)
A Cornish 0-suffix pet-form of CHRISTOPHER.

LALLOW
Found as the Christian name of at least two early 16th century Cornishmen. Menheniot church is dedicated to St. Lalluwy, whose name, according to Charles Henderson - is found corrupted to LALLOW in 1500.

LEW
PN - RS Old Cornish name the Old Welsh

name LLEU, 'guide', 'ruler'.

LEWYTH
PN - RS Old Cornish name = the Old Welsh name LLYWEITH, 'ruler'. Found inscribed on a Camborne altar-stone and recorded as a Cornish word in a 12th century glossary of Cornish words.

LOCRYN
A not uncommon Christian name in pre-18th century Cornwall.

LOWTHAS
PN (Pron. with the 'th' soft as in 'then') RS Old Cornish name = the Old Welsh name LLEUDDAD.

LUK
(Pronounced 'leek') The Middle Cornish form of the name LUKE.

LYWARGH
PN (Pron. 'loo-arh') A RS Old Cornish name = the Old Welsh name LLYWARCH.

MABAN
PN An Old Cornish name = the Old Breton name MABAN, possibly a derivative of MAB, 'son'.

MADERN
A saint, probably Welsh, who gave his name to Madron, near Penzance. The not uncommon surname MADDERN preserves the older form of the name. Cf. the surnames GLUYAS and BIDDICK.

MALSCOS
PN - RS Old Cornish name = the Old Breton name MAELSCUET, from MAEL, 'prince', and SCUET 'shield'. The surname TREVASKIS contains this name.

+MANUEL and EMANUEL
Hebrew, 'God with us'. Although essentially a Spanish and Portuguese name, EMANUEL and its shortened form MANUEL enjoyed considerable popularity in pre-18th century Cornwall.

MARGH
(Pron. 'marh') The Cornish form of MARK, by way of British from Latin MARCUS. Found in the play 'Bewnans Meryasek' and as a placename element.

MASEK or MADOK
PN (Pron. 'mazz-ek'/'mad-DOK') RS Old Cornish name corresponding to the Welsh name MADOG, which has long been a favourite Welsh Christian name. There is much to be said for preferring the Middle Cornish placename form of the name, MASEK, which is unlikely to be mistaken for the Welsh name.

MASSEN

The name of a traditional Cornish king in the play 'Bewnans Meryasek'.

MAWGAN

A British saint who gave his name to St. Mawgan-in-Pyder and to Mawgan-in-Meneage. The name is from British MAGLOCUNOS, 'lofty / mighty prince'. Although MALGAN would be more correct, it was as MAWGAN that 17th century Cornishmen bore the name.

MAYEK or MAYOK

PN Prof. Loth believed that the name FEOK is a corruption of MAYOK. MAYOK, from British MAGIACOS, corresponds to the Old Breton name MAIOC and seems to occur in at least one placename. See FEOK.

MELOR

May have survived until the 16th century where it appears as MELLIOR.

MERYASEK

(Pronounced 'murr-YAZZ-ek') St. Meryasek is the subject of the play in Cornish, 'Bewnans Meryasek', 'Life of Meryasek'. Although patron of Camborne, St. Meryasek is now perhaps best known in Brittany, where his name takes the form MERIADEK.

MERYN

PN - RS Old Cornish name = the Old Welsh name MERIN and the Old Breton name MEREN. It seems likely that the church at St. Merryn was originally dedicated to a male missionary who bore this name.

MERYEN

PN (Pron. to rhyme with 'Veryan') RS Old Cornish name =
the Old Welsh name MERIAWN and the Old Breton name
MERION, from Late Latin MARIANUS.

MEWAN

A saint according to tradition a Welshman, who
gave his name to St. Mewan. Cf. the Breton
saint's name MEVEN.

MODRED

The Modred of Arthurian romance. In Cornwall
the name is found as a Bodmin Manumissions
name and as a placename element, e.g. in
CARVEDDRAS (KAER VODRES, 1342). The name has been
left in its Old Cornish form.

+MORLEY
Popular in Cornwall over a long period.

MYGHAL
(Pron. 'ma-HAIL) A Middle Cornish form of MICHAEL found in Middle Cornish literature. Occurs as MEHALE, etc., in at least two late placenames.

MYRGHAL
Was in use as a Christian name in the 16th century when it was spelt MYHELL.

MILYAN
The name of a legendary ruler of Cornwall and also a Bod. man. name. The name-saints of Mullion and of St. Mellion may have borne this name, which is apparently from Late Latin AEMILIANUS.

MILYEK or MILYOK
PN - RS Old Cornish name, probably from Latin AEMILIACUS.

NADELEK
(Pron. 'no-DELL-ek') Cornish, 'Christmas Day'. Occurs in the extinct Cornish surname NADELACK, which suggests that the name may have been used as a Cornish equivalent of NOEL.

NERTH
Cornish, 'strength'. May occur as a nickname in the placename TRENARTH.

NEYTHEN
PN (Pron. 'nigh-thun') The Cornish form of the Irish name NECTAN, which, as the name of a saint, is perpetuated in St. Nectan, near Lostwithiel. The name seems to occur in several placenames, but is possibly for EYTHYN, 'furze-bush', in some cases.

NICCA
Apparently a 'Cornish' pet-form of NICHOLAS.

NOY
Cornish for nephew; recorded as a St Just Christian name in the 17th century.

OMFFRA or OMFRA
A pre-16th century colloquial form of HUMPHREY. Old English HUNFRITH.

+OTES
Old German AUDO, later ODO or OTHO, a derivative of AUDA 'rich'. ODO and OTHO crossed the channel with the Normans and are found as OTES in later medieval England. In Cornwall OTES and OTTY are found up to the early part of the 17th century.

PADERN
According to tradition, St. Padern was a Cornish chieftain and father of St.

Costentyn. He is patron of North and South Petherwin. The name is from Latin PATERNUS.

PASCO(W)

The accepted view is that the name is from Cornish PASK, 'Easter', with a Cornish -O/-OW suffix meaning 'of'. If this is correct, PASCOW is the Cornish counterpart of the obsolete English name PASCAL and of the surviving Breton name PASCOU. An alternative suggestion, based on the theory that the -O/-OW suffix had a diminutive function, is that PASCOW is a diminutive of the obsolete English name PASK, which had the same meaning as the Cornish word. PASCOW was a fairly common name for Cornish boys until the first few decades of the 18th century.

PASCUS

Popular in Cornwall in the 17th century.

PAWLY

A fairly common 17th century form of PAUL.

PAWLYN

PN - RS Old Cornish name from Latin PAULINUS.

PEDER

(Pron. 'pay-dur') The Cornish form of PETER. The spelling PEDYR is encountered as frequently as the spelling PEDER.

PENCAST

Cornish, 'Whitsuntide', 'Pentecost'. The Christian name PENTECOST, from the Greek word for Whitsuntide, was in general use until the 17th century, when it became rare and increasingly associated with Cornwall, where it survived until the end of the last century. The Cornish name for Whitsuntide is found as a surname (e.g. Saundry Pencaste, St. Ives, 1605) and may have been used as a Christian name.

PEDREK or PETHEREK

Petherick and Peddrick are recorded as Cornish Christian names up to the first quarter of the 18th century and seem to preserve the otherwise unrecorded Middle Cornish form of Petrok, *PEDREK. Cf 14th century forms of the placename Trebetherick.

PERAN or PERRAN

The saint who gave his name to Perranzabuloe, Perranporth, Perranworthal and Perranuthnoe. Patron of Cornish miners and acclaimed by many as Patron Saint of Cornwall. As a Christian name PER(R)AN seems to have survived until the beginning of the 19th century. The spelling PIRAN, leading inevitably to the pronunciation 'pie-ran', is incorrect and is based on the erroneous identification of St. Per(r) and with a quite different saint.

PETROK

St Petrok vies with St. Peran for the title of Patron Saint of Cornwall. Probably from South Wales, he settled at what is now Padstow (Petrok's stow) His name, which corresponds to the Welsh name PEDROG, was used as a Christian name by pre-18th century Cornishman. The form PEDROK would be nearer the sound of his name in Old Cornish, but PETRO(C)K seems to be too well established to tamper with.

RAW

A colloquial form of RALPH current in pre-18th century Cornwall. Ralph, from Old English RAEDWULF (=Old Norse RATHULFR). A compound of RAED 'counsel' and WULF 'wolf', was later reinforced by Norman influence. It developed into RAUF or RAFF, which were the usual forms of the name until the 17th century. Carew (1555-1620) regarded RAW as the Cornish counterpart of RAFE, the standard form of the name by his time.

RAWLYN

A diminutive of RAOUL, the French form of RADULF. Not uncommon outside Cornwall in the Middle Ages. Survived in Cornish use until the latter part of the 16th century if not later.

REMFRY

Old German RAGANFRID, a compound of RAGAN 'might' and FRITHU 'peace'. RENFRED crossed the Channel with the Normans and was fairly common elsewhere up to the 16th century. In its usual Cornish form, REMFRY, the name became obsolete in the last century, but as RENFRED it still survives as Cornish Christian name.

+ RENOWDEN

Old English REGENWEALD, a compound of REGEN and WEALD, both of which mean 'power', 'force'. After the Conquest the name was reinforced by Norman REYNAUD, of which RENOWDEN is a diminutive. The name still survived in Cornwall at the beginning of the 18th century.

REWAN (RUMON)

St. Rewan / Rumon gives his name to Ruan Lanihorne and to other places in Cornwall and Devonshire. The discrepancy between REWAN (or RUAN if preferred) and RUMON is explained by the fact that Old Cornish had a weakly nasal 'V' which sounded something like an 'm'. Since there was no letter in the Latin alphabet to represent 'v','m' was used in its place. Rewan preserves the later colloquial (and more correct) form of the name. The name also occurs in the Bod. man.

RYEL or RYOL

(Pron. 'ree-el'/ 'ree-ol') Found as a Bod. man. name, as the name of a traditional

Cornish king in the play 'Bewnans Meryasek', and as a possible placename element. Possibly from British RIGALIS.

SADORN
PN - RS Old Cornish name, from Latin SATURNUS, 'Saturn'. The word for 'Saturday' in Cornish.

SALAN
An Old Cornish name found in the Bod. man. and probably in the placename CARSELLA (KARSALAN, 1086).

+SAMSON
Hebrew, 'child of Shamash' (the sun-god). The name of the champion of the Israelites and of a Welsh bishop who passed through Cornwall on his way to Brittany. He is patron of Golant and gave his name to one of the Isles of Scilly. Once fairly common everywhere, SAMSON became virtually obsolete after the Reformation. Still survives in Cornwall.

SEBASTIAN
See BASTIAN

SANTO
A Cornish O-suffix pet-form of ALEXANDER.

SELEVAN
(Pron. 'se-LEV-vun') The Cornish form of SOLOMON. St. Selevan gave his name to St. Levan and is said to have been the father of St. Keby.

SILYEN (Properly SULYEN)
The original patron of Luxulyan. SILYEN = the Old Welsh name SELIEN and the Old Breton name SULENN, from SULGENOS, 'sun born'.

SITHNY
The saint who gave his name to Sithney is the same person as the Breton St. Sezni.

TALAN
An Old Cornish name found in the Bod. man. and as a placename element TALAN = the Old Breton name TALAN and is a derivative of TAL, 'forehead'. Possibly the unknown name-saint of Talland.

TALEK
A Cornish adjective meaning 'big-browed' which may account for the surname TAL-LACK. A suitable first name.

TANGY or TANGUY

(Pron. 'tann-gee') This Breton Christian name was introduced into England by Breton followers of the Conqueror, and is especially common as a surname in eastern England. Cornish bearers of the surname may be descended from the Breton labourers, artisans and curates who settled in medieval Cornwall. The name is still fairly common in Brittany as a Christian name and means 'fire dog'.

TEUDAR or TEWDAR

The pagan tyrant in the Cornish play 'Bewnans Meryasek' and the traditional enemy of the early Christian missionaries in Cornwall. His name (or that of another Teudar) survives in the St. Kevern placename LESTOWDER, 'court (of) Teudar'.

TREEVE

Popular in Cornwall today; may originate from the place of that name.

TRYSTAN or TRISTAN

The hero of medieval romance, nephew of King Mark of Cornwall, lover of Eseld. The name is thought to derive from DRUSTAN, a known British name which later became influenced by French TRISTE, 'sad'. TRISTAN seems to occur in the placename TREDRESTAN and may be preserved, in its older form, in the inscription on the famous inscribed stone, at Menabilly. TRISTRAM, TRUSTRAM and TRISTRAN are medieval English perversions of the name and are not suitable for Cornish use.

TUDWAL

PN - RS Old Cornish name = the Middle Welsh name TUDWAL, from British TOTO-UALOS, 'people powerful'.

TUDY

(Pron. 'tew-dee') A little-known saint who gave his name to the parish of St. Tudy.

UDY

(Pron. 'ew-dee') Not uncommon as a 16th century Cornish Christian name.

UNY or EWNY

An obscure Celtic saint who is patron of Redruth and Lelant, and joint patron of Crowan. His name has been used as a Christian name.

UST

(Pron. 'east') Very little is known about the saint who gave his name to St. Just-in-Roseland and to St. Just-in-Penwith. In Cornish mouths his name from Latin JUSTUS, was pronounced 'east'.

UTHER

Occurs in l6th and 17th century parish registers. A legendary king of the Britons, by an adulterous association with Ygerna, wife of Gorlois, Duke of Cornwall, he became the father of Arthur, who succeeded him.

WELLA

A 'Cornish' pet-form of WILLIAM. Regarded by at least two 17th century Cornishmen as the Cornish equivalent of the name.

YESTIN

A Yestin was said to be a son of St. Gerens. The name occurs in the Bod. man. and, like Welsh IESTIN and English JUSTIN, is said to be a derivative of Latin JUSTUS.

YLLOGAN or ILLOGAN

A saint who gave his name to Illogan. Cf. the Old Breton name ILLOC from which ILLOGAN may be a derivative.

YTHEL or YETHEL

It is believed that Cornish bearers of the surname JEWELL perpetuate the name IUDHAEL, 'generous lord', which is thought to have been reintroduced by early Breton settlers. The name seems to occur in Cornish placename TRETHILL (TREYUTHEL 1393, 1394). The suggested modern form YTHEL takes into account the later development of the language and corresponds to the modern Welsh name ITHEL.

YTHGANS

PN - RS Old Cornish name = the Old Breton name IUDCANT 'white / splendid lord'.

YTHNO(W) or UTHNO(W)

The unknown missionary whose name is coupled with that of St. Peran in the placename PERRANUTHNO. The name means 'famous lord', from IUD, 'lord', and a suffix meaning 'familiar'.

Nearly all of the newly-devised compound names included are based on names current in Wales, but are sufficiently dissimiliar in form not to be mistaken for Welsh names. They are described as 'Cornish compound' to distinguish them from a single dictionary word. Like them, they are indicated by a capital 'D'.

+ANGELET
Angelet is a French feminine diminutive form of the obsolete name ANGEL, which still survives in Italy as ANGELO. From the Greek word for 'messenger'. Found in 17th century Cornish parish registers.

ARGHANS or ARRANZ
D Cornish, 'silver'. In 17th century Cornwall ARGENTINE was sometimes used as a Christian name.

+ARMYNEL
Armynel was a popular name in 17th century Cornwall. It may be a diminutive of ARMINE, the English form of French ARMAND.

ATHWENNA
Athwenna is the latinized form of ADWYN, the name of the missionary remembered at Advent, near Camelford. She is said to have been one of the daughters of the semi-historical King Brychan of Wales.

AVIS / AUYS
Popular in Cornwall in the 16th century.

BANALLEN
D (Pron. 'ba-NALL-en') Cornish, 'broom flower'.

BARENWYN
D (Pron. 'ba-REN-win') Cornish compound meaning 'fair branch'.

+BEATEN
Latin, 'bringer of joy'. A common medieval diminutive form of BEATRIX. Still survived in 17th century Cornwall.

BENNATH
D Cornish, 'a blessing'.

BERLEWEN
D (Pron. 'bur-LEW-en') Cornish, 'Venus', 'morning star'.

+BERSABA
A medieval form of BATHSHEBA which still survived in early 18th century Cornwall.

BERYAN
The name-saint of St. Buryan.

+BLANCHA / BLANCHE
Popular in Cornwall over many centuries until the present day.

BLEJAN
D Cornish, 'bloom'.

BLEJENNYK
D (Pron. 'bla-JENN-ik') Cornish, 'little bloom'.

BLEJWYN
D Cornish compound meaning 'fair flower', the Cornish equivalent of Welsh BLOD-WEN.

BORA or BORRA
D Cornish, 'dawn'.

BRONNEN
D Cornish, 'a rush'.

BRYLUEN
D Cornish, 'rose'.

CAJA
D Cornish, 'daisy'.

CATERN
Popular in the 17th century.

+CHESTEN
Old English CHRISTHEN, 'Christian'. A form of CHRISTINE in use in 17th century Cornwall.

CLORENDA
Popular in the 17th century.

COLUMBA
A feminine form of COLUM given to 17th century St. Columb girls.

CONWENNA
A name from legend. Conwenna was the daughter of a legendary ruler of Cornwall.

+CORDELIA
When used today it is probably always taken from Shakespeare's KING LEAR. The name may be the same as CORDULA, which appears in Welsh and Cornish calendars as the name of one of the companions of St. Ursula. Since CORDELIA occurs quite frequently in early Cornish parish registers, it may have been a traditional name in Cornwall .

CREWENNA
The latinized form of the name of the saint remembered at Crowan.

CRYDA or CREEDA
(Pron. 'creed-a') The patron of Creed, near Grampound. Nothing is known about her.

DELEN or DELLEN
D Cornish, 'petal'.

DELENNYK
D Cornish, 'little petal'.

DEMELZA
A placename in the parish of St. Wenn. DEMELZA has been used in recent years as a pleasant-sounding girls' name. For those who are more concerned with euphony than meaning (DEMELZA may mean 'hill-fort of Maeldaf') there are many other placenames which can be used as names for girls. E.g. LAMORNA, MORVA, LAMANVA. CLODAGH, the name of a river in Tipperary, is only one example of the scores of placenames and river names which have been used as Christian names.

DEROWEN
D (Pron. 'der-ROW-en') Cornish, 'oak'.

DERWA
Late medieval sources link St. Derwa with St. Ya. Her name is perpetuated in Menedarva, Camborne, formerly MERTHER DERWA, 'chapel (of) Derwa'.

+DONAT or DONNET
Latin, 'given'. Given to boys as well as girls in the Middle Ages, DONAT remained in Cornish use as a name for girls until as late as 1755.

+DORCUS
Popular in Cornwall in the 17th century.

DORYTY
Popular in the 17th century. Possibly a Cornish form of Dorothy.

DYWANA
The name of a legendary ruler of Cornwall.

EBREL
D Cornish, 'April'.

ELESTREN
D (Pron. 'el-LEST-ren') Cornish, 'iris'.

ELOWEN

D (Pron.' el-LOW-en') Cornish, 'elm'.

+EMBLYN

Properly EMMELINE, from Old French AMELINE. A common name in the Middle Ages. In the form EMBLYN it is still found in late 17th century Cornish parish registers.

ENDELYON

Patron of Endellion, near Port Isaac.

ENOR

D Cornish, 'honour'.

EPPOW

Occurs in the 16th century as a rare name for West Cornish girls. R Morton Nance suggested that EPPOW is a Cornish O-suffix pet-form of ELIZABETH. If so, EPPOW would have been formed from IBBET, the usual diminutive of ISABEL (LA), the French and Spanish form of ELIZABETH and one of the commonest female names in the l3th and 14th centuries. Cf. RICHOW.

ESYLD or ESELD

The heroine of the Tristan romances, wife of King Mark of Cornwall and lover of Tristan. Unfortunately, the Old Cornish form of the name has not survived in Cornish use. There can be little doubt that it occurs in HRYT ESELT, 'Eselt's ford', a lost St. Keverne placename mentioned in a charter of 967. This Old Cornish name corresponds to the Middle Welsh name ESYLLT, and would have become *ESELS or *EJELS in later Cornish use. ESELT/ESYLLT may possibly derive from a British *ADSILTIA and mean something like 'she who is gazed at'. It was a common name in the Middle Ages, owing its popularity to that of the Tristan romances. It is usually recorded in the latinized form ISOLDA, but the spoken form of the name was derived from French ISEUT, which gave rise to spellings like ISAT and ISSOT. In this form, the name was quite common in pre-l7th century Cornwall. Modern parents who wish to use the name because of its Cornish associations will no doubt prefer to avoid latinized ISOLDA and Frenchified ISEULT. The forms ESYLD and ESELD, based on Old Cornish ESELT are distinguishingly Cornish and are matched by modern Breton ISILD and modern Welsh ESSYLLT. The pronunciation of the names ESYLD/ESELD is 'ez-ZILD'/'ez-ZELD'.

+EULALIA

Greek , 'sweetly-speaking'. Fairly common in France and Spain. EULALIA names a Cornish woman when found in Britain. Now obsolete or very rare.

EVA
(Pron.'ayv-a') The Cornish form of EVE.

EWA
Although St. Ewe has been regarded as a woman since at least the 12th century, it is possible that 'she' is to be identified with the Breton male saint, St. Eo. The barton adjoining the church of St. Ewe, LANEWA, 'monastic close (of) Ewa', preserves an older form of the name.

FYNA or FEENA
D Cornish, 'finer'.

GLANDER
D Cornish, 'purity'.

GLANNA
D Cornish, 'purer'.

GONNETTA
Gonnetta is found as a 14th century name for Cornish girls. Of uncertain etymology, it may have been formed from the name of the patron of Roche.

GWAYNTEN
D Cornish, 'spring'.

GWENIVER
An older, more Cornish form of JENIFER found in some early parish registers. See JENIFER.

GWENEP
The name-saint of Gwennap.

GWENNOL
D Cornish, 'a swallow'.

GWIRYON
D Cornish, 'innocent', 'sincere'.

GWYNDER
D Cornish, 'brightness'.

HEBASCA
D Cornish, 'solace'.

HEDRA
D Cornish, 'October'.

+HESTER
Variant of the name ESTHER, but more popular in Cornwall than elsewhere.

+JAQUET

French feminine diminutive of JACQUES (JAMES). Occurs in Britain from the 13th to 17th centuries. Not uncommon in 17th century Cornwall.

JENIFER

The Welsh name GWENHWYFAR, the name of King Arthur's wife, is believed to account for Anglo-Norman GUENIEVRE, which became GAYNORE or GWENORE in the later English romances. In the forms GUENER and GUEANOR it survived in Lancashire until the beginning of the 17th century. Most authorities believe that the name entered Cornwall as Anglo-Norman GUENIEVRE, but there are others who maintain that the name may have enjoyed a continuous and independent existence in Cornwall from the earliest times, and that its survival in the heartland of Arthurian tradition owes nothing to the Anglo-Normans. JENIFER (found as GWENIVER in some early parish registers) became appreciably commoner in some parishes in the 18th century, at the very time so many old favourites were disappearing, and is Cornwall's only native name to achieve popularity in Britain as a whole. It is now so common that most people have ceased to regard it as a Cornish name. Cornish tradition seems to uphold the spelling JENIFER.

JENIFRY

Seems to be a Cornish form of WINIFRED. ST. GWENFREWI was said to have been a Welsh princess martyred by Caradoc. The latinized form of her name, WENEFREDA, was anglicized as WINIFRED, and was sometimes confused with the Old English masculine name WINFRITH. That JENIFRY is not a corruption of JENIFER is apparent from the occurrence of the name in the form JENEFRED. JENIFRY is presumably from an earlier Anglo-Norman GUENIFROI. Cf. JENIFER and REMFRY.

JENNA, JEDNA and JANA

Seem to be pre-17th century West Cornish forms of JANE, from Old French JEHANE. All three forms seem to have been influenced by the West Cornish linguistic background and may be comparable with other Cornish A-suffix names like WELLA and HICCA.

JOWANET

A diminutive of JOAN (earlier JOHAN), the usual feminine form of JOHN. Fairly common in the earlier West Cornwall parish registers. In the Cornish speaking area of Cornwall, JOWANET seems likely to have been regarded as an appropriate feminine equivalent of JOWAN, the Cornish form of JOHN. Spellings like GEWANATT and JEWANATT, which follow the Late Cornish pronunciation of JOHN, seem to support this suggestion.

JOWNA

A pre-17th century colloquial form of JO(H)ANNA or possibly a cornicised form of JOHAN, the earlier form of JOAN. Cf. JENNA

KAYNA, KEYNA or KEYN

St. Keyn, or to give her one of the latinized forms of her name, KAYNA, is the patron of St. Keyne and is one of the better known Cornish saints, owing much of her fame to Southey's humorous poem 'The Well of St. Keyne'. She is said to have been one of the Children of Brychan. Her name may be derived from Welsh CAIN, 'beautiful'.

KEKEZZA (Properly KYKESOW)

D Cornish, 'heath'. The best Cornish equivalent of the name HEATHER.

KELYNEN

D (Pron. 'ke-LINN-en') Cornish, 'holly'.

KENSA

D Cornish, 'first'.

KERENSA or KERENZA

(Pron. 'ke-RENZ-a') Cornish, 'affection', 'love'. The name is already in use.

KERESEN or KEREZEN

D (Pron. 'ke-REZZ-en') Cornish, 'cherry'.

KERESYK or KEREZIK

D (Pron. 'ke-REZZ-ik') Cornish, 'dear'.

KERRA

D Cornish, 'dearer'.

KEWA or KEW

Nothing is known about the name-saint of St. Kew, near Wadebridge, except that she was reputed to be the sister of DOCCO, the name of a Glamorgan saint.

KEWERA or KEWERAZ

D (Pron. 'ke-WERR-az') Cornish, 'fulfil-ment', 'perfection'.

LASEK or LADOK

(Pron. 'lazz-ek'/'ladd-OK') Practically nothing is known about the saint who gave her name to Ladock. (This placename made the transition from LADOC to LASEK but has since reverted to LADOCK).

LOVEDAY or LOWDY

A common medieval Christian name which has now become confined to Cornwall, where it still survives in occasional use. The name was originally bestowed on boys or girls on a LOVEDAY, a day appointed for a meeting between enemies and litigants with a view to an amicable settlement. Now given only to girls, the name takes the colloquial form LOWDY in some earlier parish registers.

LOWENA or LOWENNA
(Pron. 'lo-WENN-a') Cornish, 'joy'. Already in use as a name.

LOWENEK
D (Pron. 'lo-WENN-ek') Cornish, 'joyful'.

MABENA
(Pron. 'ma-been-a') The latinized form of MABYN. Although the patron of St. Mabyn, near Wadebridge, is traditionally a woman, and was depicted as such in the old St. Neot church windows. It seems possible that she may have been a man with a name corresponding to the Old Welsh name MABAN.

+MARIOT
Hebrew, probably, 'wished-for-child'. The usual diminutive form of MARY in the Middle Ages. Survived in Cornwall as late as 1725.

MARYA
(Pron. 'ma-REE-a', like Italian MARIA) The Cornish form of MARY. The late 17th century Cornish writer William Rowe used the spelling MAREEA.

MELDER
D Cornish, 'honey-sweetness'.

+MALLONEY or MELANIE
Greek, 'black'. As MELANIA, borne by two Roman saints. MELANIE is popular in France and probably crossed the Channel with Huguenot refugees. Recorded in Cornwall and Devonshire from the 17th century, MELANIE is still in use in Cornwall, where the traditional spelling of the name is MELLONEY. Although regarded as primarily Cornish on this side of the Channel, it is probably no longer possible to separate Cornish tradition from modern French influence.

MELWYN
D - Cornish compound meaning 'honey-fair'.

MELYONEN
D (Pron. 'mell-YONN-en') Cornish, 'violet'.

MELYOR or MELIORA
Exclusively Cornish in distribution and possibly a corruption of a native Celtic

name, MELIORA is first recorded in 1218. Very common as MELYOR/MELLEAR in 17th and early 18th century parish registers, the name survived for a while in the last century, generally in the form MELIORA.

MERAUD or MEROUDA

This Cornish name is usually taken to be a contraction of Middle English EMERAUD, 'emerald', but is recorded as MEROUDA as early as 1296, which is earlier than the first recorded occurrence of EMERAUD. It has been suggested that MERAUD is a native Cornish name, possibly a derivative of MOR, 'sea'.

METHEVEN

D (Pron. 'me-THEVV-en') Cornish, 'June'.

MORGELYN

D Cornish, 'sea-holly'.

MORENWYN

D (Pron. 'mor-RENN-win') A Cornish compound meaning 'fair maiden'.

MORVATH

Used in the 17th century, possibly from an earlier form of the place name Morvah.

MORVOREN

D (Pron. 'mor-VORR-en') Cornish, 'maid of the sea', 'mermaid'.

MORWENNA

The name-saint of Morwenstow (Morwenna's stow). MORWENNA is already in use.

MORWENNOL

D Cornish, 'a sea-swallow', 'tern'. (The sea bird).

NESSA

D Cornish, 'second' or 'nearest'.

NEWLYNA

(Pron. 'new-LEEN-a') The latinized form of the name of the saint who is remembered at Newlyn, near Newquay.

NONNA or NON

Patron of Altarnon and Pelynt. Very little is known about the real St.Nonna.

PASCA, PASCATTE, PASCES, PASCOWES
Are all feminine forms of the once common Cornish masculine Christian name PAS-COW, which derives from Cornish PASK, 'Easter'.

PESWERA or PEZWERA
D (Pron. 'pez-WERR-a') Cornish, 'fourth'.

+PETERNELL
Popular in Cornwall in the 17th century.

PRUDENS
A Cornish form of Prudence.

+REDIGAN
A fairly common pre-18th century name for Cornish girls. It seems (for an alternative etymology has been suggested) to be the feminine name RADEGUND, from the Old German RADAGUNDIS, a compound of RADI 'counsel' and GUNDI 'war'.

RICHOW
A fairly common pre-17th century name for Cornish girls. The name does not seem to occur in standard reference books; it is perhaps a feminine pet-form of RICHARD, with a Cornish -OW suffix used in a diminutive capacity.

ROSEN or ROZEN
D (Pron. 'rozz-en') Cornish 'rose'.

ROSENWYN
D (Pron. 'roz-ZENN-win') A Cornish compound meaning 'fair rose'.

SENARA
The latinized name of the patron of Zennor. Nothing is known about her.

SIDWELL
Latin SATIVOLA, possibly a latinization of an Old English name. St. Sidwell is the patron of Laneast church, near Launceston, and of a parish in Exeter. Nothing is known about her. The name occurs in the 16th and 17th centuries as a rare name for Cornish girls.

SOWENA or SOWENNA
D (Pron. 'so-WENN-a') Cornish, 'success'.

SPLANNA
D Cornish, 'brighter'.

STEREN
D Cornish, 'star'.

STERENNYK
D Cornish, 'little star'.

TALWYN
D - Cornish compound meaning 'fair brow'.

TAMARA
A name from folklore. According to Robert Hunt (Popular Romances of the West of England, 1871), TAMARA was a nymph who gave her name to the Tamar.

TAMSYN
The usual medieval feminine diminutive form of THOMAS. Properly THOMASINE, TAMSYN was once a very popular name for Cornish girls. It became less fashionable in the 18th century but still survives in occasional Cornish use. Because of its obsolescence elsewhere, it is now generally regarded as a Cornish name.

TECCA
D Cornish, 'fairer'.

TEGEN
D Cornish, 'ornament', 'pretty little thing'.

TREGERETH
D (Pron. 'tre-GAIR-eth') Cornish, 'mercy', 'compassion'.

TRESSA
D Cornish, 'third'.

TRUETH
D (Pron. 'troo-eth') Cornish, 'compassion'.

UGHELLA or EWELLA
D (Pron. 'yoo-ELL-a') Cornish, 'higher', 'more exalted'.

WENNA
St. Wenn is the name-saint of the parish adjoining St. Columb and is also patron of Morval church. Her name is GWEN, 'white / splendid', which also happens to he the first element in GWENDOLYN. Since the abbreviation GWEN is fairly common, latinized WENNA has been preferred.

WHECCA
D Cornish, 'sweeter'.

WHEGYN
D Cornish, 'sweet or dear little one'.

WYLMET or WILMOT

A feminine diminutive of WILLIAM. Fairly common in the earlier parish registers. Has been revived in this century.

YA

(Pron. 'ee-a') The name of the saint who gave her name to St. Ives, formerly PORTH YA, 'Ya's port'.

YGERNA or IGERNA

A name from Arthurian legend. The wife of Gorlois, Duke of Cornwall, and mother of Arthur.

YSELLA

D (Pron. 'iz-ZELL-a') Cornish, 'more modest/unpretentious'.

+ZENOBIA

The name of a famous queen of Palmyra. For some reason it came into use in late 16th century Cornwall. It may still survive. Occurs as ZONOBY in some parish registers. SINEY seems to be a pet-form of the name.